JINGDEZHEN

TOUR GUIDE 2025

Explore Jingdezhen: Top Destinations, Travel Tips, and Unforgettable Experiences for 2025

Ige Maraag

Table of Contents

INTRODUCTION

1.1 Overview of Jingdezhen

Jingdezhen, frequently referred to as the "Porcelain Capital" of the world, is a city located in the northeastern section of Jiangxi Province, China. Renowned for its nearly 2,000 years of history in porcelain production, Jingdezhen stands as a symbol of China's rich ceramic heritage. This city is set between the lush mountains and the flowing rivers of the region, presenting a picturesque landscape that compliments its artistic past.

Jingdezhen's popularity dates back to the Han Dynasty (206 BC - 220 AD), but it was during the Tang (618-907 AD) and Song (960-1279 AD) Dynasties that the city began to acquire its renown for creating excellent porcelain. The city's pottery achieved new heights under the

Ming (1368-1644) and Qing (1644-1912) Dynasties, being highly sought after by both domestic and international markets. The Qing Dynasty saw the zenith of Jingdezhen porcelain manufacturing, with the city being the imperial kiln for the Chinese court, producing porcelain items that were coveted by emperors and collectors alike.

Today, Jingdezhen continues to be a center of porcelain manufacturing, with many factories and artisan workshops still following ancient methods passed down through generations. The city integrates its old porcelain-making techniques with modern technology, assuring its place in both history and the contemporary world of ceramics.

1.2 Importance of Jingdezhen in China's Cultural and Historical Landscape

Jingdezhen maintains a unique and vital role in China's cultural and historical environment. Its significance is mostly connected to its contribution to Chinese art and craftsmanship, particularly in the domain of porcelain. Porcelain, frequently dubbed "china" in the West, is one of China's most important cultural exports, and Jingdezhen's role in this extends far beyond basic manufacture. The city was home to the imperial kilns during many Chinese dynasties, and its porcelain works have played a crucial role in Chinese diplomacy and trade for millennia.

Throughout history, Jingdezhen's porcelain functioned as both a luxury item and an artistic expression. Its delicate, often intricately painted decorations, notably during the Ming and Qing Dynasties, were appreciated for their skill and beauty. These porcelain works were not only sold domestically but were also traded over the Silk Road and abroad, reaching markets in Europe, the Middle East, and Asia. As a result, Jingdezhen became an important hub for both creative innovation and international trade.

The city's relationship with porcelain is not merely a narrative of economic triumph but also one of cultural exchange. The designs, techniques, and patterns utilized in Jingdezhen ceramics have influenced art across the globe, producing an enduring legacy that continues to touch contemporary ceramic artists. In recognition of its historical value, much of Jingdezhen's kilns, factories, and antiques are protected as part of China's national heritage.

1.3 Purpose and Scope of the Guide

The objective of this book is to provide a thorough and insightful resource for anybody interested in discovering Jingdezhen, whether for cultural enrichment, creative inquiry, or travel delight. This book tries to discover the numerous facets of the city, offering a deep dive into its history, cultural sites, art, local food, natural landscapes, and more.

The scope of this guide spans not only the city's rich heritage but also its present-day energy. We will discover Jingdezhen's historical and cultural sites, its world-class museums and art galleries, the local culinary scene, the wide range of shopping experiences, and possibilities for outdoor activities. Additionally, the tour will touch on events and festivals, providing you insight into the vivid celebrations and traditions that take place throughout the year.

Whether you are an art fan, history buff, nature lover, or simply a curious visitor, this book is meant to help you plan an engaging and fulfilling visit to Jingdezhen.

1.4 What to Expect in This Guide

This book is structured into chapters, each concentrating on a major part of the Jingdezhen experience. Throughout, we present not just practical information but also historical background, cultural relevance, and advice to enhance your understanding and appreciation of the city.

Getting to Know Jingdezhen: Learn about the city's remarkable history, cultural significance, and its continuous association with porcelain craftsmanship.

Planning Your Trip: Discover the best dates to visit, how to get to Jingdezhen, and ideas on accommodations, transportation, and budgeting.

Historical & Cultural Landmarks: Explore major historical landmarks that have defined the city's identity, including ancient kilns, temples, and heritage buildings.

Art and Museums: Delve into the artistic culture of Jingdezhen with information on museums, galleries, and artisan workshops.

Culinary Delights and Drinks: Indulge in local delicacies and learn about the distinct food culture that makes Jingdezhen's culinary offerings stand out.

Outdoor Adventures & Natural Escapes: Uncover the natural splendor around Jingdezhen, from hiking paths to peaceful lakes and mountains.

Shopping and Souvenirs: Discover where to buy original Jingdezhen porcelain and other unique local crafts.

Festivals and Events: Gain insight into the festivals, cultural performances, and festivities that exhibit the city's rich traditions.

Exploring Beyond Jingdezhen: Extend your adventure to nearby cities and scenic regions worth seeing.

Practical Information: Essential guidance about local customs, language, emergency services, and how to make the most of your vacation.

Each chapter is organized to deliver clear and useful information, ensuring you are well-prepared for every element of your trip.

1.5 Tips for First-Time Visitors

For visitors visiting Jingdezhen for the first time, here are some practical tips to ensure a seamless and enriching experience:

Learn Basic Mandarin Phrases: While many individuals in Jingdezhen can speak in Mandarin, learning a few simple phrases like "Hello" (你好, Nǐ hǎo) and "Thank you" (谢谢, Xièxiè) will go a long way in making your encounters more enjoyable.

Respect Local Customs: Chinese culture is profoundly founded on respect and friendliness. Be careful of local norms, such as offering and taking gifts with both hands and avoiding public expressions of wrath or irritation.

Wear Comfortable Shoes: Whether you're touring the porcelain workshops, hiking in neighboring mountains, or exploring historical landmarks, you'll do a lot of walking. Comfortable footwear is key.

Prepare for the Weather: Jingdezhen experiences a subtropical climate with hot, humid summers and moderate winters. Pack accordingly, and consider packing a water bottle, sunscreen, and an umbrella for sudden rain showers.

Take Time to Explore the Art: Jingdezhen's porcelain workmanship is a marvel to behold. Don't speed around the galleries and seminars. Take time to admire the exquisite designs and historical significance behind each piece.

Bargain Respectfully: In markets and smaller shops, bargaining is usual. While it's expected, always do so with respect and a friendly attitude.

Be Mindful of Local Time and Holidays: China celebrates numerous major festivals, including the Lunar New Year, when many establishments may close. Plan accordingly, especially if you're traveling during the high Christmas season.

With this advice and insights, you are ready to start on a wonderful adventure through one of China's most culturally diverse and historically significant cities.

GETTING TO KNOW
JINGDEZHEN

2.1 A Brief History of Jingdezhen

Jingdezhen's historical roots reach back over two millennia, making it one of China's oldest and most prominent towns in terms of both culture and industry. Its link with porcelain dates back to the Han Dynasty (206 BC - 220 AD), yet it was during the Tang Dynasty (618-907 AD) that the city began to earn renown for its ceramic industry. The word "Jingdezhen" itself, which means "town of porcelain," came into general usage during the Song Dynasty (960-1279 AD), signifying the city's growing renown as a hub for ceramic creativity.

The Ming (1368-1644) and Qing (1644-1912) Dynasties were periods of extraordinary prosperity for Jingdezhen. During these periods, the city became the site of the imperial kilns, where porcelain for the imperial court was made. These porcelain items were not only utilized within China but were also exchanged throughout the Silk Road and sent to Europe, the Middle East, and other regions of Asia, strengthening Jingdezhen's importance in international trade.

The city's porcelain industry has traditionally been highly appreciated for its remarkable quality, commonly seen in delicate white porcelain with exquisite blue-and-white motifs. Over the centuries, Jingdezhen became synonymous with excellent ceramics, its status as a ceramic production center extending through dynasties and beyond.

2.2 Geographic and Cultural Context

Jingdezhen is situated in the northeastern portion of Jiangxi Province, China, surrounded by lush mountains, rivers, and rolling hills. This geographic location not only makes it a gorgeous destination but also has historical value. The city is located near the Gan River, a key waterway in the region, which historically enabled the movement of both raw materials for porcelain production and finished products to other parts of China and abroad. The region's rich natural resources, particularly high-quality kaolin clay, and sufficient water, were important for the city's growth as a porcelain production powerhouse.

Culturally, Jingdezhen has been a junction of influences from numerous Chinese dynasties and beyond. The interplay of native customs with those from other places has generated a unique cultural blend in the city. The local people take enormous pleasure in their long-standing ceramic legacy, and the entire city seems to breathe porcelain, from the murals on buildings to the artists at work in the workshops. Jingdezhen's lively culture also incorporates influences from Buddhism, Taoism, and local folk traditions, with temples, festivals, and art profoundly entwined in the city's character.

2.3 The Rise of the Porcelain Industry

The emergence of the porcelain industry in Jingdezhen is connected with the city's geographical and cultural evolution. The region's abundance of natural resources made it perfect for porcelain production. One of the fundamental elements for porcelain production is kaolin clay, which was found in abundance near the city, giving rise to its world-renowned porcelain industry.

The skill of porcelain production was improved over centuries in Jingdezhen, with the development of methods such as glazing, molding, and painting becoming extremely advanced by the time of the Tang and Song Dynasties. Under the Ming and Qing Dynasties, Jingdezhen became the epicenter of porcelain artistry, supplying the imperial court with fine porcelain pieces that were both utilitarian and decorative. These porcelains generally had exquisite designs, from floral patterns to depictions of mythical animals, and were highly coveted for their smooth texture and translucent clarity.

Jingdezhen's significance in the porcelain industry was not merely a home triumph; it became a significant part of world trade. The city's porcelain was exported to the West, especially during the Ming and Qing Dynasties, influencing European ceramic manufacture. Jingdezhen's blue-and-white porcelain became particularly famous, with European collectors referring to it simply as "china." The city's porcelain production remained unparalleled in quality and craftsmanship, and even today, the city continues to be a major hub for ceramic art, attracting artists, collectors, and tourists alike.

2.4 Local Traditions and People

Jingdezhen's residents are intimately tied to the city's pottery traditions. For generations, the locals have been involved in all stages of porcelain production, from mining and processing raw materials to shaping, glazing, and firing the ceramics. This hands-on engagement with the city's trade has developed a strong sense of pride in the local community.

The traditions of porcelain production are passed down from generation to generation. Many families in Jingdezhen have been involved in the ceramic trade for decades, and the skills of the art are often passed down within families. Artisans in the city are not only competent in traditional skills but are also very innovative, mixing current designs with ancient ways. Visitors to Jingdezhen often have the chance to witness these craftspeople at work, learning about the various processes involved in porcelain production.

Beyond ceramics, Jingdezhen's inhabitants have a rich cultural legacy that encompasses diverse folk practices. Local festivities, such as the Lantern Festival and the Dragon Boat Festival, offer vivid performances and processions, contributing to the city's cultural vibrancy. Traditional music, dancing, and storytelling continue to be part of life in the city, frequently highlighting the region's deep connection to nature and spirituality.

2.5 Economic and Social Landscape Today

In recent times, Jingdezhen has been a prospering city that has managed to blend its rich historical history with contemporary economic development. The city remains a leader in the porcelain sector, with many ceramic companies still running and manufacturing high-quality porcelain. The porcelain sector not only drives the local economy but also supports several other businesses, including tourism, retail, and education.

Tourism is one of the primary drivers of Jingdezhen's contemporary economy. Visitors from all over the world flock to the city to explore its rich history, visit the local workshops, and witness the craftsmanship of porcelain creation firsthand. The city has invested in presenting itself as a cultural tourism destination, with the creation of museums, galleries, and historical sites displaying its rich heritage in pottery. The Jingdezhen Ceramic Culture and Art Museum and the Jingdezhen Ceramic Institute are among the significant organizations that reflect the city's cultural and educational commitment to maintaining its past while also supporting innovation in ceramic arts.

Socially, the city has undergone substantial growth and modernization, yet it has managed to keep much of its original beauty. While the younger generation is rapidly turning toward more diverse vocations, many continue to work in the ceramics business, keeping the craft alive. The city also faces the issues of development, such as managing visitor influxes and balancing modernity with cultural preservation.

Overall, Jingdezhen stands as a tribute to the endurance of its people and its ability to adapt while honoring its ancient past. With its continued significance in the worldwide ceramics industry, rich cultural legacy, and thriving local traditions, Jingdezhen remains one of China's most unique and culturally significant cities.

PLANNING YOUR TRIP

3.1 Best Time to Visit Jingdezhen

The best time to visit Jingdezhen depends on the type of experience you want to have and the weather conditions that suit you best. Generally, the most opportune time to visit the city is during the spring (March to May) and fall (September to November) months, when the weather is moderate and agreeable. During these seasons, temperatures range from 15°C to 25°C (59°F to 77°F), making it suitable for exploring outdoor attractions, visiting porcelain factories, and attending local festivals without the inconvenience of excessive heat or cold.

Winter (December to February) is also a wonderful season for travelers who want fewer crowds and don't mind the cold weather. Temperatures can drop to roughly 5°C (41°F) or lower, and the city tends to be quieter as many tourists avoid the winter chill. While some outdoor activities may be less pleasurable during the colder months, winter is still a perfect time to immerse yourself in the cultural attractions and interior art displays without the bustling crowds.

The summer months (June to August) can be hot and humid, with temperatures often topping 30°C (86°F). This is also the busiest tourist season, notably during the Chinese National Holiday in early October, so be prepared for greater crowds and higher hotel expenses. Although summer offers an opportunity to experience Jingdezhen's bustling atmosphere, you may wish to pack light clothing, sunscreen, and plenty of water to keep comfortable in the heat.

3.2 Travel Essentials

Visa: Most overseas travelers will need a visa to enter China. Depending on your nationality, you may need to apply for a tourist visa (L visa) at a Chinese embassy or consulate before your travel. The visa normally enables stays of up to 30 days. It's vital to apply well in advance to minimize delays. Be sure to check the latest visa requirements on the official Chinese embassy website for your country, as these sometimes fluctuate.

Currency: The official currency in China is the Chinese Yuan (CNY), commonly known as the Renminbi (RMB). As of now, 1 USD is about equal to 7 CNY, though exchange rates might fluctuate. ATMs are generally available in Jingdezhen, and most major credit cards (Visa, MasterCard) are accepted in hotels, large businesses, and restaurants. However, tiny establishments and rural locations may only accept cash. It's suggested to convert some currency before your trip or upon arrival at the airport or local exchange bureaus.

Language: The major language spoken in Jingdezhen is Mandarin Chinese. While many younger people working in tourism-related businesses may grasp some basic English, most locals, especially in marketplaces and smaller shops, may not speak English fluently. Learning a few key phrases in Mandarin, such as "Hello" (你好, Nǐ hǎo) and "Thank you" (谢谢, Xièxiè), can assist boost your experience and interactions. It's also a good idea to carry a translation software or phrasebook for ease.

3.3 Transportation Options

Getting to Jingdezhen: Jingdezhen is well connected by numerous modes of transportation. The nearest major airport is Jingdezhen Luojia Airport (JDZ), which serves domestic flights to and from major cities like Beijing, Shanghai, and Guangzhou. From the airport, you may easily reach the city center by taxi or airport shuttle. For foreign passengers, planes normally transit through Beijing Capital Foreign Airport (PEK) or Shanghai Pudong International Airport (PVG), and then a connecting flight to Jingdezhen is necessary.

If you prefer going by train, Jingdezhen is accessible by the high-speed rail network. The city boasts a modern railway station, Jingdezhen Railway Station, which connects it to major cities including Nanchang, Hangzhou, and Wuhan. Train travel in China is efficient and economical, and high-speed trains can be a comfortable and scenic way to travel.

For passengers coming by bus, Jingdezhen has a sophisticated transportation system that links the city with adjacent cities and provinces. Long-distance buses are available at the Jingdezhen Long-Distance Bus Station, and buses are a cost-effective choice for tourists on a budget.

Getting Around Jingdezhen: The city boasts a reliable public transit system, including buses and taxis. Buses are a cheap way to move around, with services covering key tourist destinations, shopping regions, and industrial zones. However, public buses might be busy during peak hours, and schedules may not always be published in English, so it's a good idea to ask locals for instructions if needed.

Taxis are convenient and reasonably inexpensive, with metered prices based on distance. Most cabs do not have English-speaking drivers, so it's helpful to have your destination printed in Chinese. Additionally, for those who prefer more flexibility, renting a bicycle or e-scooter is a popular and eco-friendly method to explore the city at your leisure.

For more isolated places or specific tourist destinations, such as the porcelain workshops, booking a private tour or using a ride-hailing app like Didi (China's counterpart of Uber) may be a better alternative.

3.4 Accommodations

Jingdezhen offers a selection of hotel alternatives, appealing to varied budgets and preferences. Whether you're looking for a luxury hotel, a mid-range guesthouse, or a budget-friendly hostel, you'll find a location that matches your needs.

Luxury Hotels: Jingdezhen's luxury lodgings are mainly found in international hotel chains or newly developed boutique hotels. These hotels frequently offer comfortable rooms, modern facilities, and services like airport shuttles, Wi-Fi, and breakfast. Popular luxury hotels include the Jingdezhen Grand Hotel and the Jindu Hotel.

Mid-Range Hotels: For travelers seeking comfort at a more modest price, mid-range hotels offer exceptional value for money. Many of these hotels are strategically positioned, making it easy to visit nearby attractions and retail districts. Examples include the Shangri-La Hotel Jingdezhen and local favorites like the Jingdezhen International Hotel.

Guesthouses & Hostels: For a more local and intimate experience, guesthouses and hostels give budget-friendly options for travelers. Many of these lodgings are family-run and offer a warm ambiance, along with the chance to engage with local folks. Common options include boutique guesthouses in traditional buildings or tiny hostels in central districts, giving communal or individual rooms.

3.5 Budgeting Your Trip

Jingdezhen is a very economical vacation, especially when compared to China's bigger cities like Beijing or Shanghai. However, your final expenses will depend on the type of trip experience you desire to have.

Accommodation: Budget tourists should expect to pay roughly 100-300 CNY (15-45 USD) per night for a dormitory bed in a hostel or a cheap guesthouse room. Mid-range hotels typically cost between 300-600 CNY (45-90 USD) per night for a double room. Luxury hotels can cost upwards of 600 CNY (90 USD) per night.

Food: Local food in Jingdezhen is inexpensive, with dinners at modest eateries or street sellers costing approximately 10-30 CNY (1.5-5 USD). Mid-range restaurants may charge 50-100 CNY (7-15 USD) per person for a dinner. High-end eating experiences can cost more, although the total cost of meals is quite low compared to larger cities.

Transportation: Public transportation and taxis are relatively affordable. Bus rates range from 1-3 CNY (0.15-0.45 USD) per journey, whereas taxis normally start at roughly 10 CNY (1.5 USD) for a short trip. If you plan on using ride-hailing services or private excursions, expect to pay a bit more, especially for longer trips.

Sites: Entrance fees to popular sites like the Jingdezhen Ceramic Culture Museum or porcelain workshops normally cost between 20-80 CNY (3-12 USD). Special exhibitions or guided tours may require additional fees.

Overall, Jingdezhen is a fantastic location for anyone looking for a budget-friendly, culturally rich trip, with a variety of options available for all types of travelers. Proper planning and budgeting will help you make the most of your vacation while experiencing the city's historical and artistic treasures.

HISTORICAL AND CULTURAL LANDMARKS

Jingdezhen is a city steeped in rich history and cultural value, and its historical and cultural landmarks reflect its deep-rooted past. From ancient kiln sites to spiritual temples, these landmarks not only highlight the city's long-standing link with porcelain manufacture but also offer insight into its rich cultural landscape. In this section, we will explore some of the main landmarks that make Jingdezhen a fascinating trip for history and culture fans.

4.1 Jingdezhen Ancient Kiln Site

One of the most notable historical landmarks in Jingdezhen is the Jingdezhen Ancient Kiln Site, which stands as a witness to the city's millennia-long history of porcelain production.

The site is home to a variety of antique kilns that stretch back as far as the Tang Dynasty (618–907 AD), illustrating the progression of ceramic production processes throughout time. The Ancient Kiln Site is located just outside the city center and is a huge complex of antique kilns and workshops. Visitors can experience a range of kiln types, including those used for firing early porcelain as well as those from later periods when ceramic manufacture became more industrialized. The site offers a view into the intricate and labor-intensive process of porcelain manufacture in ancient times, allowing visitors to appreciate the craftsmanship and inventiveness involved.

Many of the kilns at the site have been scrupulously kept, with some still preserving remnants of ancient pottery and porcelain. The site is not just an archeological gem but also a valuable educational resource, with various museums and exhibitions providing insight into the history and processes of porcelain production. Guided tours offer in-depth information about the importance of these kilns in shaping Jingdezhen's status as the "Porcelain Capital" of China.

4.2 Porcelain Culture Museum

The Porcelain Culture Museum in Jingdezhen is another major monument that gives tourists a complete grasp of the city's artistic and historical significance. Located near the core of the city, the museum is committed to preserving and showcasing Jingdezhen's rich porcelain heritage.

The museum houses a vast collection of porcelain antiquities, spanning from early ceramic pieces manufactured during the Tang and Song Dynasties to more contemporary works created by modern artists. Among its features are the famed blue-and-white porcelain pieces that Jingdezhen is known for, as well as delicate pottery and porcelain artifacts manufactured for the imperial court during the Ming and Qing Dynasties.

The museum is organized into multiple display halls, each concentrating on a different aspect of porcelain culture, including the production process, design processes, and the progression of porcelain styles over time. One of the museum's most fascinating displays is the display of porcelain fragments and kiln tools that have been unearthed from the old kiln sites in the vicinity. Additionally, the museum organizes regular workshops and demonstrations where visitors can observe expert artisans produce porcelain products using traditional methods.

By visiting the Porcelain Culture Museum, tourists acquire a fuller awareness of Jingdezhen's significance as the cradle of porcelain craftsmanship, with an opportunity to observe firsthand how the city's porcelain manufacture has influenced global art and commerce for centuries.

4.3 Taoist and Buddhist Temples

Jingdezhen is home to various Taoist and Buddhist temples that reflect the city's significant cultural and spiritual legacy. These hallowed sites are not only noteworthy for their religious significance but also provide an insight into the historical development of local architecture and art.

The Longquan Taoist Temple, located on the outskirts of the city, is one of the most renowned Taoist temples in Jingdezhen. This temple is dedicated to Taoist deities and is recognized for its serene environment and exquisite traditional architecture. The temple contains various rooms and pavilions embellished with elaborate carvings and paintings, making it a quiet sanctuary for both locals and visitors alike. The temple's surrounding grounds also allow tourists to explore nature and reflect in a tranquil environment.

Another noteworthy religious building is the Fohua Buddhist Temple, which dates back to the Song Dynasty. The temple is notable for its large architectural design, with many courtyards and traditional Buddhist statues. The temple is still actively used for religious events and festivals, and visitors can experience the activities of local Buddhist communities. The Jingdezhen Buddhist Museum, located nearby, displays a collection of Buddhist relics and sacred objects, providing further insight into the importance of Buddhism in the region's history.

These temples not only serve as places of worship but also as cultural icons, with many visitors going to these sites to experience the spiritual peace they offer while learning about Taoist and Buddhist traditions that have affected the city's culture for generations.

4.4 Ancient Streets and Buildings

Jingdezhen's historical appeal extends beyond its kilns and temples to its antique streets and buildings, many of which have been preserved for centuries. Walking through the tiny streets and passageways of the city conveys a sense of the old-world charm that has remained essentially intact throughout the years.

One of the most prominent sites in the city is Old Street (Gucheng Lu), a busy marketplace that has served as the focus of commerce and trade in Jingdezhen for generations. The street is dotted with classic architecture, including ancient merchant houses, courtyards, and shopfronts, many of which have been turned into modern ceramic workshops, galleries, and cafes. Visitors can wander the street to discover the blend of old and new, as artists preserve the historic history of porcelain making while simultaneously catering to the current tourism business.

The Jingdezhen Ancient City Wall is another historical wonder worth viewing. While much of the wall has crumbled over time, sections of it still survive as a reminder of the city's strategic importance during the Ming Dynasty. The wall was originally designed to safeguard the city and its rich porcelain manufacturers against future invasions. Today, tourists can stroll along the remaining sections of the wall and enjoy views of the surrounding environment, including the local rivers and mountains.

These ancient alleys and buildings provide a window into the past, offering tourists an opportunity to experience the city's historical atmosphere while discovering the rich culture and heritage that built Jingdezhen.

4.5 The Cultural Significance of Porcelain

Porcelain in Jingdezhen is more than just a craft; it is an intrinsic aspect of the city's character and cultural significance. For over a thousand years, Jingdezhen has been the epicenter of porcelain production in China, and its influence on global ceramics is immense. The city's porcelain items, famed for their delicate craftsmanship, exquisite glazes, and elaborate designs, have been highly appreciated by both the imperial court and collectors worldwide.

The cultural significance of porcelain extends beyond its material value, it reflects the city's artistic spirit and skill. In traditional Chinese culture, porcelain has been regarded as a symbol of refinement, elegance, and beauty. The process of porcelain manufacture itself is considered an art form, blending the elements of nature-earth, water, and fire with human ability and creativity. In this sense, porcelain production in Jingdezhen is regarded as a type of cultural expression, embodying not just technical expertise but also philosophical concepts relating to harmony, balance, and beauty.

Today, Jingdezhen's porcelain tradition is maintained and honored through its museums, cultural landmarks, and festivals. The city continues to be a hotspot for contemporary ceramic artists, and modern porcelain pieces that merge old techniques with innovative ideas are highly recognized both domestically and abroad. Visitors to Jingdezhen can experience the cultural richness of porcelain firsthand, learning about its historical significance while seeing its continuous progress as a Chinese art form.

Jingdezhen's historical and cultural sites offer an immersive trip into the city's rich heritage. From the old kilns and porcelain museums to the spiritual temples and historical streets, these landmarks reflect the deep cultural and artistic significance of porcelain in shaping Jingdezhen's identity and its long impact on the globe.

ART AND MUSEUMS

Jingdezhen, frequently referred to as the "Porcelain Capital" of China, is not only a hub for traditional ceramic manufacture but also a booming center for contemporary art and ceramic innovation. The city's deep relationship to porcelain artistry is mirrored in its museums, galleries, and dynamic art venues, where both traditional techniques and current interpretations of ceramics come to life. This section discusses the important art institutions in Jingdezhen, the role of ceramics in the city's identity, and the chances for tourists to engage with interactive art experiences.

5.1 The Jingdezhen Ceramic Art Museum

The Jingdezhen Ceramic Art Museum is one of the major institutions in the city, dedicated to demonstrating the history, workmanship, and artistic progression of ceramics. Established in the early 21st century, the museum serves as a primary resource for individuals interested in the delicate skill of porcelain manufacture and the culture around it.

The museum's collections span a large range of periods, from early Tang Dynasty ceramics to the modern-day advances in porcelain. The displays include porcelain relics that represent Jingdezhen's contributions to Chinese art, such as excellent blue-and-white porcelain, imperial porcelain ceramics, and pieces that reflect regional and foreign influences over the years.

A highlight of the museum is its extensive presentation of porcelain production processes, providing visitors an opportunity to appreciate the complexity and creativity involved in creating porcelain from raw materials to final items.

In addition to historical items, the Jingdezhen Ceramic Art Museum also showcases contemporary ceramic art. Many current Chinese ceramic artists and international artists whose work merges traditional and creative techniques are often shown. The museum's rotating exhibitions offer a unique opportunity to witness how ceramic art has changed over time, as well as to discover the new paths it is taking in the 21st century.

5.2 Contemporary Art Spaces and Galleries

Beyond conventional porcelain, Jingdezhen has been home to a rising number of modern art spaces and galleries, where local and international artists explore numerous mediums, including ceramics, sculpture, installation art, and mixed media. These spaces reflect the city's developing reputation as a creative hub for modern art.

One of the prominent contemporary art venues is The Jingdezhen International Ceramic Art Village, a unique environment dedicated to ceramic art experimentation and artistic collaboration. The art village brings together both local craftspeople and foreign artists who explore the linkages between traditional porcelain techniques and current artistic practices. The village provides seminars, exhibitions, and artist residencies, giving a dynamic setting where art forms flourish, and new ceramic techniques are born.

Additionally, tiny galleries in the city center, such as Gao Cheng Art Gallery and Zhoujia Art Gallery, display contemporary ceramic pieces that represent the artists' interpretations of Jingdezhen's porcelain tradition. These locations generally focus on abstract and philosophical works, pushing the frontiers of ceramic art while also respecting its rich historical roots.

Jingdezhen's contemporary art scene is flourishing rapidly, with several galleries routinely organizing shows that blend traditional and modern ceramic works. The city's blend of old techniques and forward-thinking art makes it an exciting trip for people interested in both historical and modern ceramic expressions.

5.3 Traditional Pottery Workshops and Studios

No visit to Jingdezhen is complete without visiting the traditional ceramic workshops and studios that maintain the centuries-old craft of porcelain manufacture. These studios are where the magic of ceramic creation happens, and many of them provide interactive opportunities for visitors to get hands-on with ceramics and learn from professional artisans. The city is home to various historic pottery factories where tourists may witness expert artists at work, crafting everything from superb porcelain vases to delicate figurines. Some businesses, like Jingdezhen Porcelain Factory and Laozi Pottery Studio, offer guided tours that dive into the history of porcelain production and explain the step-by-step process of converting raw clay into exquisitely sculpted porcelain.

For those interested in more hands-on experiences, many of the programs allow guests the opportunity to try their hand at pottery making. These interactive courses allow you to create your pottery, led by experienced local artisans. You can learn about the subtleties of shaping clay, the numerous varieties of glazes, and the firing process that makes Jingdezhen porcelain so unique. These experiences are not only a terrific opportunity to learn about the craft but also offer a personal connection to the city's rich ceramic culture.

5.4 The Role of Ceramics in Jingdezhen's Identity

Ceramics are intimately woven into the identity of Jingdezhen, impacting its cultural environment, business, and daily life. The city's link with porcelain extends back more than 1,000 years, and the evolution of porcelain as both an art form and a commodity has defined much of its history.

Jingdezhen's porcelain industry has won it a place in the global arena, and its name is synonymous with superb ceramic craftsmanship. The city's reputation for making high-quality porcelain has garnered royal support throughout the dynasties, particularly during the Ming and Qing periods, when Jingdezhen-produced porcelain was desired by emperors and nobility.

Today, porcelain continues to be a fundamental component of the city's character. It is not simply a traditional craft but also a source of pride for the inhabitants, who regard their work as a reflection of both their cultural legacy and their artistic ingenuity. The city's porcelain culture is a vital aspect of its tourism economy, attracting art collectors, historians, and tourists eager to experience the artistry of the city firsthand. Jingdezhen's ceramic art industry also gives livelihoods to thousands of craftsmen, potters, and small business owners, ensuring that the craft remains a living, thriving aspect of the city's identity.

5.5 Opportunities for Interactive Art Experiences

For those looking for more than simply passive observation, Jingdezhen provides several options for participatory art experiences that allow tourists to engage directly with the city's dynamic artistic community.

In addition to pottery-making courses, there are various ceramic art festivals and interactive exhibitions presented throughout the year. The Jingdezhen International Ceramic Festival, for example, welcomes ceramic artists from around the world and provides interactive activities where attendees can engage in workshops, lectures, and collaborative art projects. These festivals create a dynamic, immersive setting where visitors can not only learn but actively contribute to the creative process.

Many local art studios also offer "make-your-own" pottery experiences, where tourists may design their personalized porcelain mementos, which are then fired and glazed by the craftspeople. These experiences allow travelers the ability to depart Jingdezhen with a significant, handmade piece of art that symbolizes the city's cultural legacy.

Additionally, tourists can attend art demonstrations at several museums and galleries, where artisans and artists explain their creative process, from making elaborate porcelain designs to developing new ceramic techniques. These presentations provide an in-depth insight into the workmanship and artistry involved in ceramic creation, providing for a hands-on, immersive cultural experience.

Jingdezhen offers a wealth of art and museum experiences that display its historical and modern ceramic talent. Whether exploring the enormous collections of the Ceramic Art Museum, visiting modern galleries and workshops, or engaging in interactive pottery-making activities, visitors can immerse themselves in the artistic energy of this wonderful city. Ceramics in Jingdezhen are not merely a craft, they are a living heritage and a key component of the city's cultural fabric, giving an exceptional experience for art lovers and cultural enthusiasts alike.

CULINARY DELIGHTS AND DRINKS

Jingdezhen, a city famed for its porcelain, also provides a distinct culinary environment that blends classic Chinese dishes with local specialties, rich tea culture, and contemporary dining experiences. Food aficionados visiting the city may indulge in varied dishes, experience the time-honored tea culture, and discover famed street food while also enjoying exquisite dining at some of the city's greatest restaurants. This section emphasizes the crucial cuisine experiences you should not miss when in Jingdezhen.

6.1 Local Specialties & Dishes to Try

Jingdezhen's food culture is profoundly steeped in Jiangxi province's culinary traditions, with distinct flavors that reflect the region's agricultural riches. The most famous meal to try in Jingdezhen is Jingdezhen rice noodles (景德镇米粉), a cherished local specialty. These thin rice noodles are often served in a hot broth with various toppings like braised pork, pickled vegetables, and fresh herbs. The noodles are light and delicate, giving them a fantastic introduction to the city's cuisine.

Another must-try local meal is Jiangxi-style fish head (江西鱼头), a dish where the fish head is cooked with rich, fragrant broths created from local ingredients, including chili peppers and Sichuan peppercorns. The resulting flavor is both spicy and aromatic, frequently savored with steamed rice.

For those who prefer savory snacks, Jingdezhen-style dumplings (景德镇饺子) are a favorite street food. The dumplings are filled with a range of foods, such as pork, veggies, or shrimp, and are recognized for their thin, soft exterior and tasty contents. These dumplings can be boiled or fried and are commonly served with a side of dipping sauce.

Additionally, Lushan rice cakes (庐山米糕) are another local dish worth tasting. These sticky, chewy rice cakes are seasoned with a blend of sweet and savory ingredients and are generally served as a light snack or dessert after a meal.

6.2 Traditional Jingdezhen Tea Culture

Tea occupies a significant position in Jingdezhen's history, and the city's historical affinity with porcelain continues its tea culture, as Jingdezhen is famed for creating beautiful teapots and tea sets. Chinese tea culture is a vital aspect of life in the city, with numerous local tea rooms allowing visitors the chance to enjoy traditional tea rituals and try a wide variety of teas.

One of the greatest ways to drink tea in Jingdezhen is by visiting a tea house, where you may taste locally sourced teas such as Jiangxi Green Tea (江西绿茶) and Black Tea (红茶). These teas are often served in high-quality porcelain teapots, allowing visitors to appreciate the blend of artistry and tradition in every cup.

The Wulong Tea Ceremony, which is popular in Jingdezhen, is an immersive experience for tea connoisseurs. Guests at the tea ceremony can learn about the art of brewing tea, from the meticulous selection of leaves to the precise temperature at which the water should be poured. The ceremony also provides an opportunity to experience the ritualistic character of Chinese tea culture, which is oriented around balance, peace, and respect for the environment.

Some tea shops, such as Gongfu Tea House, also provide private tea tastings, where visitors can explore the intricacies of different tea kinds and learn how to produce the perfect brew. The tea culture in Jingdezhen is intricately entwined with its porcelain past, creating a holistic experience for those who enjoy both tea and the brilliance of ceramic production.

6.3 Famous Street Food and Market Finds

Street food in Jingdezhen is bright and tasty, with a wide choice of savory snacks, sweet desserts, and local delicacies available at markets and along the city's bustling streets. Jingdezhen Night Market is a fantastic spot to experience a range of street food items, from grilled skewers to freshly baked pancakes.

One popular street meal is baozi (包子), steamed buns filled with either savory pork or sweet ingredients such as red bean paste or lotus seed paste. These buns are an inexpensive and delightful snack, great for savoring while strolling through the city's markets.

You should also look out for chuanr (串儿), skewered meats that are barbecued over an open flame. Vendors frequently provide a variety of selections, including chicken, beef, and lamb, marinated with local spices and chili before being grilled to perfection. The crispy and delicious skewers are frequently served with a dusting of sesame seeds and chili powder.

For a sweet treat, try tangyuan (汤圆), little glutinous rice balls packed with sweet fillings such as sesame paste or red bean paste. These delicacies are often consumed during festivals but may be available year-round in many local shops.

6.4 Best Restaurants for Fine Dining

While Jingdezhen is famed for its street food, the city also provides a range of fine dining venues where guests can have a refined experience with high-quality foods made by top chefs.

One of the top restaurants in the city is The Porcelain Garden Restaurant, located in the heart of Jingdezhen. The restaurant offers a fine environment with a wide menu that incorporates a blend of traditional Jiangxi flavors and modern culinary techniques. Dishes like steamed fish with ginger sauce and braised pork belly with pickled mustard greens are beautifully cooked, providing a contemporary take on classic Chinese cuisine.

For a more personal eating experience, Jingdezhen Peking Duck Restaurant delivers some of the greatest Peking Ducks in the neighborhood. The restaurant's distinctive duck dish is cooked using traditional ways, with crispy skin and soft flesh, often accompanied by thin pancakes, hoisin sauce, and fresh vegetables.

Laozhou Garden Restaurant is another fantastic option for those wanting an elegant dining experience. The restaurant specializes in Jiangxi cuisine, featuring delicacies such as braised river fish and eggplant with garlic sauce, all presented in an attractive atmosphere.

6.5 Food Experiences in Ceramics-Themed Venues

In Jingdezhen, cuisine and ceramics are strongly intertwined, and several dining places include ceramics-themed locations that merge the two arts in unusual ways. Many of these venues feature handcrafted Jingdezhen porcelain teacups, plates, and serving vessels, allowing visitors to appreciate not only the food but also the workmanship of the city's ceramic artists.

A famous example is The Kiln Restaurant, which is set in a building meant to imitate an ancient porcelain kiln. The restaurant serves a range of traditional cuisines, with each meal presented on beautifully carved porcelain plates, giving visitors a feeling of the city's artistic history while dining. The inside incorporates ceramics artwork and pottery-making demonstrations, adding to the entire experience.

Additionally, some ceramic workshops in Jingdezhen have set up cafes or modest dining spaces where guests may have a meal while observing craftspeople at work. These locations allow you to experience both the manufacture of ceramics and the culinary delights of the region in a pleasant, creative atmosphere.

Jingdezhen's culinary scene offers a diversity of experiences that reflect the city's cultural past. From its native specialties like rice noodles and dumplings to its rich tea culture and dynamic street food scene, there's something for every pallet. Fine dining restaurants and ceramics-themed food outlets provide an extra layer of elegance and creative flair, making Jingdezhen a location where food and art come together to create remarkable experiences.

OUTDOOR ADVENTURES AND NATURAL ESCAPES

Jingdezhen, tucked in the picturesque province of Jiangxi, is not just a paradise for porcelain fans but also a gateway to stunning natural landscapes and outdoor adventures. The surrounding region offers a variety of adventures for nature lovers, from exploring majestic mountains and calm lakes to hiking through lush woods and enjoying eco-tourism. In this part, we explore some of the most intriguing outdoor activities and natural getaways around Jingdezhen, as well as how the city's natural environment has inspired its ceramic traditions.

7.1 Mount Huangshan Day Trips

A day trip to Mount Huangshan (黄山), or Yellow Mountain, is one of the favorite outdoor adventures for visitors to Jingdezhen. Located about 2 hours by vehicle from the city, Huangshan is one of China's most famous and stunning mountain ranges, famed for its iconic granite peaks, ancient pine trees, and mysterious clouds that often cloak the peaks in a dramatic haze.

The area offers a wide selection of trails for hikers of all levels, with paths leading to spectacular vistas, calm temples, and tranquil lakes. The West Sea Grand Canyon walk is a famous route, recognized for its stunning cliffs and panoramic panoramas. Those interested in a less demanding climb can opt for the cable car journey to the summit of the mountain, affording broad views of the surrounding area.

In addition to the hiking opportunities, Huangshan is also home to various cultural treasures, including ancient temples and the famed Jinshan Temple, where tourists may enjoy both the natural beauty of the mountain and the historical significance of the region.

Huangshan's particular beauty and cultural heritage have made it a popular topic for Chinese artists, notably several ceramic designers from Jingdezhen, who have drawn inspiration from the landscape's peaceful and rugged beauty.

7.2 Scenic Walks and Hikes Around Jingdezhen

Closer to Jingdezhen, there are several scenic hikes and hiking paths that allow tourists to immerse themselves in the region's natural splendor. Wuyi Mountain, approximately an hour's drive from the city, offers a selection of routes that wind through lush forests, bamboo groves, and riverbank scenery. This mountain is famed not only for its stunning beauty but also for its biodiversity, with a large array of plant and animal species to uncover.

The Jingdezhen Ceramic Culture Park is another destination worth investigating for people looking for a combination of nature and culture. Here, tourists can wander through a beautifully manicured park that merges the craft of porcelain manufacture with the natural surroundings. The park is constructed with ceramic-themed sculptures, ponds, and serene walks, giving it a peaceful refuge within the city.

Additionally, Lushan Mountain, located a bit further to the north, is a UNESCO World Heritage site recognized for its various scenery, including deep gorges, waterfalls, and ancient temples. A choice of routes here provides varied levels of difficulty, with some bringing you past historical monuments, such as the Lushan Villa, while others explore unspoiled natural beauty in the surrounding forests.

7.3 Eco-Tourism Opportunities and Nature Reserves

Jingdezhen and its surrounding areas are becoming increasingly known for their commitment to ecotourism and sustainable travel. Poyang Lake Nature Reserve, located to the north of the city, is one of the largest freshwater lakes in China and an important stop for migratory birds. The reserve offers boat trips and bird-watching possibilities, allowing visitors to explore wetlands and marshes while witnessing the vast wildlife that makes the area home.

For those interested in rural eco-tourism, the Yunshan Eco-Community is an innovative rural retreat where tourists may experience farming life while learning about sustainable agricultural practices. The community is dedicated to promoting environmental conservation, and guests can participate in activities such as organic farming, fishing, and trekking through the surrounding countryside.

Qingjiang River, another popular eco-tourism attraction in Jingdezhen, offers magnificent river cruises and trekking possibilities along its banks. Visitors can enjoy the clean waters and thick flora, making it a soothing and nature-filled way to escape the rush and bustle of the city.

7.4 Exploring Rivers and Lakes

Rivers and lakes play a vital role in the natural landscape around Jingdezhen, offering a variety of outdoor pleasures, from relaxing boat cruises to exhilarating aquatic activities. The Gan River, which runs through the region, is the lifeblood of Jingdezhen and a focal point for numerous outdoor hobbies.

Visitors can enjoy leisurely boat trips on the Gan River, where they can take in the calm waterside beauty while learning about the river's significance to the local porcelain industry. The river was once a key transportation route for porcelain exports, and its banks were formerly lined with kilns and workshops.

Poyang Lake, as indicated before, is another wonderful site for water-based activities. The lake's tranquil ambiance makes it suitable for kayaking and paddleboarding, while its wide wetlands are good for bird watching, particularly during the migratory season when thousands of species pass by.

For a more adventurous experience, the Jiangxi Eco-tourism Scenic Area offers sports including fishing and boating on crystal-clear lakes surrounded by lush forests. This area is noted for its natural beauty and serene environment, making it a fantastic place for travelers seeking a peaceful nature retreat.

7.5 The Influence of Nature on Local Ceramics

Nature has always been a significant influence on Jingdezhen's ceramics, inspiring many of the city's most famous porcelain patterns. The natural surroundings of the region, from the mountains to the rivers, have offered limitless inspiration for the exquisite designs and motifs that adorn Jingdezhen porcelain. Flowers, birds, and landscapes are common motifs in the city's ceramic creativity, representing the natural flora and animals.

Many of the motifs featured on Jingdezhen porcelain were inspired by the surrounding natural environments. Artists often include imagery of the towering peaks of Mount Huangshan, the dense forests, and the placid waters of nearby rivers and lakes in their works, capturing the beauty of the region in porcelain.

The natural resources near Jingdezhen, including local clay and mineral deposits, have also played a vital role in the porcelain-making process. The region's large resources of kaolin clay, which is needed for high-quality porcelain production, have made it feasible for artists to create beautiful, lasting ceramics that are both utilitarian and decorative.

Jingdezhen provides a multitude of outdoor adventures and natural getaways for anyone wishing to explore the region's gorgeous surroundings. Whether you're climbing through the spectacular peaks of Mount Huangshan, cruising along the Gan River, or enjoying the calm of Poyang Lake, the area's natural splendor is guaranteed to fascinate you.

Additionally, nature's influence on Jingdezhen's porcelain workmanship offers a greater awareness of the city's creative traditions, making the outdoors an integral component of the Jingdezhen experience.

SHOPPING AND SOUVENIRS

Jingdezhen is not only the capital of Chinese porcelain but also a dynamic shopping destination where visitors can discover magnificent souvenirs, real ceramics, and local handicrafts that reflect the rich cultural legacy of the city. Whether you are a collector of fine porcelain or simply searching for a unique gift to take home, Jingdezhen offers a choice of shopping opportunities. This section emphasizes the finest places to shop, what to look for, and how to navigate the world of Jingdezhen ceramics and local goods.

8.1 Where to Buy Authentic Jingdezhen Porcelain

Jingdezhen is world-renowned for its porcelain, and purchasing authentic pieces is one of the main reasons people visit the city. To acquire the best-quality ceramics, come to Ceramic Street (景德镇陶瓷街), a bustling market that specializes in high-end porcelain. Here, you may find a large choice of porcelain products, including excellent tea sets, vases, and artistic plates, all created using ancient methods passed down through centuries.

For true, museum-quality pieces, visit the Jingdezhen Ceramic Art Museum and its related stores, which offer curated collections of porcelain produced by master artisans. The museum itself highlights the history and growth of Jingdezhen ceramics, and its gift store has a superb variety of luxury porcelain pieces that reflect both historical and contemporary trends.

Additionally, the Old Kiln Workshop Area, near the Ancient Kiln site, is a good area to purchase porcelain directly from local artists and workshops. The things sold here frequently include more rustic, hand-made styles, allowing visitors a chance to take home something uniquely distinctive and crafted with local creativity.

8.2 Shopping at Local Markets and Artisan Stores

Beyond the main porcelain shopping locations, Jingdezhen includes a range of small markets and artisan stores where you may discover both traditional and modern ceramics, as well as various local products. Jingdezhen Night Market is an attractive site for casual shopping looking for a wide selection of goods, including pottery, textiles, and locally created foods. The night market is particularly bustling in the evening, with sellers offering a mix of ceramics and handcrafted jewelry, making it a fantastic location to stroll, purchase, and absorb the local vibe.

For those looking for a more artisanal experience, artisan businesses in the city's older areas offer one-of-a-kind, hand-painted ceramics and pottery that are typically not accessible in larger markets. These smaller boutiques often offer objects manufactured by local artists who are continuing the traditional traditions that made Jingdezhen famous. You can discover beautiful porcelain teacups, intricately sculpted vases, and even miniature sculptures that reflect the city's ancient ceramic legacy.

Another fantastic shopping experience is visiting the Jingdezhen Ceramic Industrial Park, where visitors can observe ceramics being manufactured in real time and purchase goods straight from the makers. Many establishments here provide personalized items, such as custom-designed teapots and plates, allowing you to make a genuinely unique gift to remember your journey by.

8.3 Souvenir Ideas

When shopping for souvenirs in Jingdezhen, ceramics are the obvious choice, but many more local handicrafts make for fantastic gifts or personal recollections. Ceramic Tea Sets are among the most popular souvenirs, ranging from simple cups and teapots to complex sets with detailed, hand-painted patterns. These tea sets may serve as both useful items and ornamental things, making them excellent for collectors or those looking to introduce a little of Chinese culture into their homes.

For something more personal, consider purchasing ceramic figures or miniature hand-painted vases that exhibit the distinctive artistry of Jingdezhen's ceramic masters. These objects are generally inspired by local landscapes, folklore, or Chinese mythology, and they come in a range of styles—from traditional to contemporary.

Aside from ceramics, local fabrics and handmade handicrafts such as embroidered silk scarves, traditional Chinese paper lanterns, and wooden sculptures are also fantastic gifts. These crafts generally contain intricate patterns and designs that represent both the cultural and environmental characteristics of the Jiangxi region.

Another interesting souvenir option is local culinary goods, such as Jingdezhen tea or preserved fruits, which are sometimes marketed in elegant porcelain vessels. These food items make for excellent and culturally rich presents that capture the flavors of the region.

8.4   Understanding   the   Craftsmanship Behind Jingdezhen Porcelain

Jingdezhen porcelain is recognized for its exceptional craftsmanship and exquisite designs, which have been developed over generations. Understanding the history and processes behind these objects might increase your shopping experience and appreciation for the artistry involved. Jingdezhen porcelain is primarily created from kaolin clay, which is highly appreciated for its purity and durability. The procedure comprises multiple technical phases, including shaping, drying, firing, and glazing.

The city's porcelain artisans commonly combine blue-and-white motifs, which are characteristic of Jingdezhen's style. These designs can incorporate delicate patterns, including flower themes, landscapes, and traditional Chinese symbols. Some modern ceramics also have colorful, multicolored glazes and contemporary designs, allowing purchasers a variety of styles to pick from.

At several local workshops, visitors may watch first-hand how the ceramics are manufactured, from the spinning of clay on the potter's wheel to the final kiln fire. This hands-on experience allows you to watch the work and dedication needed in crafting each piece. For those interested in learning more about the art of porcelain-making, various workshops offer pottery-making classes, where visitors can try their hand at creating their ceramic items under the tutelage of a master artisan.

8.5 Bargaining Tips and Local Shopping Etiquette

While Jingdezhen boasts a choice of high-end galleries and museum shops with regulated prices, haggling is a typical practice in local markets and artisan businesses. It's crucial to approach bargaining with respect and a nice attitude. Here are a few guidelines to ensure a successful buying experience:

Know the Market Value: Before bargaining, familiarize yourself with the general price range of the item you wish to acquire. This can help you avoid overpaying and offer you a basis for bargaining.

Start Low, But Be Fair: In Chinese markets, it's normal to start bargaining at a price lower than what you're ready to pay, but be reasonable. Don't seek to haggle too fiercely, as local businesses may not appreciate unfair bargaining.

Be Polite and Patient: Chinese shopping etiquette emphasizes politeness and patience. Engage in cordial conversation with the vendor, and show interest in their job. Building rapport can often lead to a better offer.

Cash is King: While many establishments accept credit cards, cash is generally preferable, and having local money (Chinese yuan) on hand can occasionally lead to a better deal.

Don't Be Afraid to Walk Away: If the price isn't right, it's acceptable to respectfully walk away. Many suppliers may contact you back with a better offer if they perceive that you're serious about leaving.

Shopping in Jingdezhen is a memorable experience that offers not only the opportunity to purchase unique and authentic ceramics but also a deeper respect for the cultural history of the city. With a diversity of marketplaces, artisan boutiques, and galleries, there's something for every taste and budget, making Jingdezhen a must-visit destination for shopping and collectors alike.

FESTIVALS AND EVENTS

Jingdezhen, popularly referred to as the "Porcelain Capital," is a city that celebrates both its rich cultural legacy and current inventiveness via different festivals and events. These occasions provide visitors with an immersive experience, highlighting the unique traditions, artistic manifestations, and religious practices of the region. From the big Jingdezhen Ceramic Festival to local seasonal celebrations, festivals in this city give an unforgettable opportunity to participate in its lively people and culture.

9.1 The Jingdezhen Ceramic Festival

One of the most famous and most anticipated events in Jingdezhen is the Jingdezhen Ceramic Festival. Held yearly, this event normally takes place in late spring or early summer, gathering ceramic aficionados, artists, collectors, and tourists from around the world. The festival highlights the city's long-standing legacy of porcelain-making and provides a platform for presenting both ancient and modern ceramic talent.

The event spans several days and involves a wide range of activities, including live porcelain demonstrations, art displays, and seminars. Visitors have the chance to see expert artists at work, shaping clay, painting exquisite patterns, and firing ceramics in traditional kilns. Local artists often offer creative designs that merge ancient techniques with contemporary aesthetics, providing viewers with an insight into the growth of Jingdezhen porcelain.

In addition to the exhibitions, the festival offers ceramic marketplaces, where local artisans and traders sell their wares, ranging from fine art porcelain to economical souvenirs. These marketplaces are a terrific opportunity to purchase real pieces, and many artists are ready to engage with visitors, discussing the history and method of their creations.

The festival also includes ceramic-related acts such as plays, music concerts, and dance performances inspired by traditional Chinese art and porcelain. Special activities, such as ceramic contests and art workshops, offer hands-on opportunities for visitors to engage in the art-making process and enhance their ceramic talents.

9.2 Cultural and Artistic Performances

Jingdezhen's festivals also promote the city's varied cultural and artistic heritage through a variety of performances that feature local talent and traditional Chinese arts. Many of these performances take place during important holidays, such as the Ceramic Festival or the

Chinese New Year, and contain aspects of Chinese opera, folk dance, and musical performances.

One significant event is the Jingdezhen Traditional Opera Festival, which commemorates the city's opera heritage with performances of regional Chinese operas, such as Jiangxi Huagu Opera. This festival combines bright costumes, dramatic performances, and live music, allowing visitors a glimpse into one of the most cherished art forms in the region.

In addition to traditional performances, Jingdezhen provides modern artistic shows that merge local culture with contemporary art. These exhibitions generally contain ceramic art, photography, digital art, and installations, reflecting the city's dynamic artistic evolution. These performances and exhibitions are held in diverse venues, including art galleries, cultural institutions, and open-air spaces, offering a diversity of experiences for people with different interests.

9.3 Religious and Seasonal Festivals

Religious festivals also play a vital role in the cultural calendar of Jingdezhen. Chinese New Year, celebrated in January or February, is one of the most important and joyous festivals in the city. During this time, the streets come alive with lion dances, dragon dances, and colorful parades. Temples across the city hold special ceremonies, giving prayers for wealth and good fortune in the new year. Many local stores and markets are decorated with red lanterns and colorful ornaments, making the entire city feel vivid and jubilant.

Another significant religious occasion is the Mid-Autumn Festival (typically observed in September), which celebrates the harvest and the full moon. People assemble to admire the moon, eat mooncakes, and participate in traditional activities like lantern parades. This festival is extremely important in Chinese culture, and Jingdezhen, with its historical link to agriculture and porcelain, commemorates it with traditional performances and community gatherings.

The Qingming Festival (Tomb Sweeping Day), traditionally observed in April, is another prominent seasonal event. During this holiday, families celebrate their ancestors by visiting their tombs and offering food and incense. It's a time for introspection and family connection, and visitors can see these practices at several local temples and historical places surrounding Jingdezhen.

9.4 Special Events Celebrating Local Traditions

Jingdezhen's unique cultural heritage is also highlighted in numerous special events throughout the year. For instance, the Dragon Boat Festival (Duānwǔ Jié) is celebrated with dragon boat races on local rivers, when teams of paddlers compete in colorful boats adorned with dragon motifs. This festival, which takes place in June, is both thrilling and rich in history, celebrating the legendary poet Qu Yuan.

Additionally, Jingdezhen's Pottery Market is an event that highlights local ceramic workmanship. Held during the spring and fall months, this market is a hub for pottery enthusiasts, where visitors can watch and buy ceramics, attend pottery-making classes, and participate in pottery workshops. It's an excellent opportunity for visitors to meet with local artists and experience the artistic culture of Jingdezhen firsthand.

The Jingdezhen Food Festival also honors local culinary traditions and educates visitors about the region's particular flavors. Held yearly, it includes a selection of food stalls, cooking demos, and tastings, providing insight into the local gastronomy. Visitors can enjoy Jiangxi's famous spicy meals, local snacks, and traditional tea culture in a colorful and stimulating atmosphere.

9.5 How to Participate in Festivals and Events

Participating in festivals and events in Jingdezhen is a fantastic opportunity to immerse yourself in the local culture and traditions. Here are a few pointers to help you make the most of your experience:

Plan: Many of Jingdezhen's festivals occur at specific periods of the year, so it's crucial to check the festival dates before your trip. This ensures that you can align your vacation with key cultural events.

Engage with Locals: During festivals, local artisans and performers are frequently eager to interact with tourists. Don't hesitate to ask questions, learn about their trades, or try participating in classes or performances.

Dress Appropriately: Some celebrations, especially religious ones, may necessitate specific clothes. If you're attending a temple ceremony or a traditional performance, be respectful by wearing proper clothing.

Be Open to New Experiences: Festivals in Jingdezhen frequently involve a blend of both traditional and contemporary cultural features. Keep an open mind, and be willing to experience new types of art, cuisine, and cultures that may be strange.

Jingdezhen's festivals and events provide a wonderful opportunity to experience the city's rich cultural past and modern artistic vibrancy. Whether you're exploring the beautiful Ceramic Festival, participating in a religious festival, or enjoying a local performance, these activities offer an enriching experience for anybody visiting the city.

EXPLORING BEYOND JINGDEZHEN

While Jingdezhen itself is a treasure trove of cultural heritage and artistic achievements, the surrounding region offers an assortment of intriguing sites for anyone wishing to explore beyond the city. From historic cities and charming villages to natural wonders and calm landscapes, the greater area of Jiangxi province is rich in attractions that appeal to varied interests. In this section, we'll examine adjacent cities, picturesque routes, and hidden gems that are worth exploring on your trip to Jingdezhen.

10.1 Nearby Cities and Attractions Worth Visiting

Several cities around Jingdezhen are steeped in history, culture, and natural beauty. Nanchang, the capital of Jiangxi Province, is a short journey away and offers a wealth of historical landmarks, including the famous Tengwang Pavilion, a classic example of ancient Chinese architecture, and the Nanchang Revolutionary Museum, which chronicles the city's role in modern Chinese history. Nanchang is also home to the picturesque August 1st Square and Qingyun Mountain, giving a fantastic blend of urban and natural adventure.

Lushan Mountain, a UNESCO World Heritage site, is another must-visit destination located around two hours from Jingdezhen. Known for its stunning views, Lushan is lined with old temples, notably Bailu Temple, and offers chances for hiking and photography. Visitors can enjoy panoramic views, waterfalls, and the quiet ambiance of this magnificent mountain, making it an ideal escape from the hustle and bustle of the city.

For those with an interest in historical architecture, Wuyuan, generally referred to as one of the most beautiful villages in China, is located to the northeast of Jingdezhen. Known for its well-preserved ancient buildings and picturesque scenery, Wuyuan is a photographer's heaven. The community is bordered by rolling hills and vivid meadows, creating a tranquil setting that feels worlds away from modern life.

10.2 Scenic Routes and Day Trips

Jingdezhen is situated in a location that is suitable for exploring picturesque routes, whether by car, train, or boat. One popular alternative for vacationers is a day excursion down the Gan River, which flows through the Jiangxi province. The Gan River offers spectacular vistas of lush green hills, historic riverside villages, and tranquil scenery. Visitors can take a boat excursion to explore the riverbanks, or simply enjoy a gorgeous drive, stopping along the way to visit small towns and local attractions.

For those wishing to experience the countryside, the Jiangxi Province Countryside Route is another wonderful alternative. This path brings travelers through attractive rural landscapes, allowing a look into the traditional ways of living in the region. Along the journey, guests can explore ancient villages, and local marketplaces, and experience some of the best rural cuisine that Jiangxi has to offer.

10.3 Exploring the Wider Jiangxi Province

Jiangxi Province is noted for its natural beauty, cultural legacy, and picturesque places. A must-visit region is Poyang Lake, the largest freshwater lake in China, located to the north of Jingdezhen. The lake is a key stop for migratory birds and a paradise for bird watching aficionados, particularly during the winter months. The neighboring area also offers stunning views and chances for boating, fishing, and photography.

Another noteworthy destination is Sanqing Peak, a Taoist sacred peak located roughly 200 kilometers from Jingdezhen. Recognized as a UNESCO World Heritage site, Sanqing Mountain is recognized for its stunning granite peaks, ancient temples, and breathtaking scenery. Visitors can trek the mountain's well-maintained trails, explore the Taoist temples, and take in views that have inspired many works of art throughout history.

The province is also home to some ancient towns and villages, such as Dongxiang, which preserve the architectural and cultural traditions of the region. These communities provide a slower pace of life and a real peek into China's rural traditions.

10.4 Nature & Adventure Beyond the City

For outdoor enthusiasts, the surrounding area offers lots of chances for nature and adventure. Tianmu Mountain is located a few hours' drive from Jingdezhen and is recognized for its diverse flora and fauna, making it an excellent site for hiking and nature treks. The area is also home to spectacular waterfalls and offers a fantastic chance for eco-tourism.

Those who prefer water-based sports will find Qiandao Lake (Thousand Island Lake) a terrific site for outdoor fun. Located in the Zhejiang Province, this enormous man-made lake offers chances for boating, kayaking, fishing, and even camping along its tranquil beaches. The lake is dotted with various islands, many of which are abandoned, providing a calm respite for nature enthusiasts and adventure seekers.

For a more unique experience, Xishan (West Mountain) is an excellent spot for exploring caves, rock formations, and natural hot springs, while also affording stunning views of the surrounding region. It's a wonderful alternative for individuals wanting both excitement and relaxation in lovely surroundings.

10.5 Hidden Gems Near Jingdezhen

Beyond the well-known attractions, Jiangxi Province is rich with hidden jewels that might give a more off-the-beaten-path experience. Fuliang Ancient Town, for instance, is a calm and attractive town located just outside of Jingdezhen. It includes classic buildings and a rich local culture that hasn't been overrun by tourism, making it a perfect location for people seeking authenticity.

Another hidden gem is the Shengjin Tower, located on the banks of the Gan River. This old tower is sometimes neglected by tourists, yet it offers spectacular views of the surrounding countryside and the river, as well as a calm hideaway for those wishing to escape the crowds.

For those interested in experiencing local village life, Yugan County is a lesser-known place that offers a look into the traditional lifestyles of rural Jiangxi. Visitors can explore local farms, enjoy traditional meals produced from fresh ingredients, and learn about the region's unique cultural practices.

Venturing outside Jingdezhen opens visitors to a multitude of opportunities to experience the diverse landscapes, cultural diversity, and hidden gems of Jiangxi Province. Whether you're drawn to the vivid history of local cities, the peacefulness of nature, or the thrill of picturesque day trips, the surrounding region provides something for every tourist. With its blend of natural beauty, historical landmarks, and untouched local gems, this area is an excellent complement to the experiences within Jingdezhen proper.

PRACTICAL INFORMATION

When planning a trip to Jingdezhen, it's crucial to have a comprehensive awareness of the practical aspects of travel, including emergency services, local customs, language, safety, and staying connected. This section will walk you through vital facts to guarantee a smooth and enjoyable visit to this intriguing city.

11.1 Emergency Contacts and Health Services

In case of emergency, it's crucial to know the local contact numbers and the locations of health services in Jingdezhen.

Emergency Numbers:

1. Police: 110
2. Fire Department: 119
3. Ambulance: 120

These numbers should be phoned in case of emergencies such as accidents, fires, or medical crises.

Hospitals and Health Clinics: Jingdezhen offers various medical facilities where travelers can seek aid if needed. Some of the most well-regarded hospitals include:

1. Jingdezhen People's Hospital (Jingdezhen Renmin Yiyuan) - A big, government-run hospital with a broad range of services, including emergency treatment.

2. Jingdezhen Traditional Chinese Medicine Hospital - For those seeking alternative treatments or traditional Chinese medicine, this

hospital offers acupuncture, herbal medicine, and more.

3. Private Clinics - There are smaller private clinics available across the city for general medical services.

Travelers should obtain travel insurance that covers medical emergencies to avoid exorbitant treatment fees in case of illness or accident. Be advised that while hospitals in larger cities are equipped with international-standard medical services, smaller clinics may have limited English-speaking staff.

11.2 Local Customs and Etiquette

Understanding and respecting local customs and etiquette is crucial to creating great encounters while visiting Jingdezhen. Here are a few crucial cultural conventions to keep in mind:

Greetings: A simple handshake is usual when meeting someone for the first time. However, other people may prefer a nod or a small bow, especially in more formal contexts.

Addressing People: Chinese people use titles to address others, and it's acceptable to use someone's professional or honorific title, such as "Mr.," "Ms.," or "Doctor," followed by their last name. First names are not typically used in official circumstances.

Respect for seniors: In Chinese society, seniors are greatly respected. Always show reverence to older folks by offering them a seat of honor, rising when they enter a room, and using courteous words.

Gifts: When offering a gift, it is traditional to offer it with both hands. Additionally, gifts are often not opened in front of the donor, as it is considered courteous to show gratitude first and store the gift for later.

Dining Etiquette: When dining, it's important to wait for the host to start the meal. Avoid sticking chopsticks upright in a dish of rice, as this mimics a burial practice. If you're toasting, it's normal to offer a drink to individuals around you.

11.3 Useful Phrases in Mandarin

While many people in Jingdezhen understand basic English, knowing a few important words in Mandarin will substantially enhance your experience. Here are some handy expressions:

Hello: 你好 (Nǐ hǎo)

Thank you: 谢谢 (Xièxiè)

Yes: 是的 (Shì de)

No: 不是 (Bù shì)

Please: 请 (Qǐng)

Excuse me: 对不起 (Duìbuqǐ) or 劳驾 (Láojià)

How much is this?: 这个多少钱？ (Zhège duōshǎo qián?)

Where is the bathroom?: 洗手间在哪里？ (Xǐshǒujiān zài nǎlǐ?)

I don't understand: 我不懂 (Wǒ bù dǒng)

Help!: 帮助! (Bāngzhù!)

Most people would appreciate the effort to speak Mandarin, and even simple pleasantries can go a long way in creating rapport.

11.4 Safety Tips for Tourists

Jingdezhen is generally considered safe for tourists, but, like any city, it's necessary to remain attentive and take care to safeguard your safety:

Keep your possessions secure: While crime rates are low, petty theft can nevertheless occur, especially in crowded venues like markets or festivals. Always keep your possessions near to you, and consider utilizing a money belt or a secured backpack.

Avoid strolling alone late at night: While Jingdezhen is a very safe city, it's a good idea to avoid poorly lit or deserted locations, particularly after dark. Stick to well-populated streets and use trusted transportation choices.

Vehicle safety: The roads in China may be chaotic, with bustling vehicles and pedestrians regularly crossing without observing signals. Always utilize pedestrian crossings and be cautious when walking on the streets.

Natural hazards: If you plan on experiencing nature or hiking, such as around the picturesque places or mountains surrounding Jingdezhen, ensure that you're sufficiently prepared. Wear suitable footwear, carry enough drink, and tell someone of your whereabouts.

Food safety: While street food might be wonderful, be cautious about eating in less reputable places to avoid foodborne infections. It's a good idea to choose kiosks or restaurants that look clean and popular with locals.

11.5 How to Stay Connected in Jingdezhen

Staying connected in Jingdezhen is pretty easy, with various choices for accessing the internet and chatting with others:

SIM Cards and Mobile Data: You can acquire a local SIM card upon arrival at the airport, train stations, or mobile phone retailers. Major carriers such as China Mobile, China Unicom, and China Telecom offer various prepaid data packages that give internet access throughout the city. Make sure your phone is unlocked and compatible with Chinese networks before acquiring a SIM card.

Wi-Fi: Many hotels, cafes, and restaurants in Jingdezhen offer free Wi-Fi. Some public venues and shopping malls also have an internet connection, though speeds may vary. It's suggested to ask for the Wi-Fi password when you arrive at a new establishment.

VPN: Since several international websites (such as Google, Facebook, and Twitter) are prohibited in China, many travelers utilize a VPN (Virtual Private Network) to breach the Great Firewall and access these platforms. Ensure that you set up a VPN before coming to China, as it can be difficult to download one while in the country.

By understanding these practical aspects of travel, you may ensure a smooth, fun, and safe stay in Jingdezhen. Whether it's knowing how to converse with people, understanding cultural etiquette, or having access to health resources, this information will help you traverse the city with ease.

CONCLUSION

Jingdezhen, regarded as the "Porcelain Capital" of China, is a city steeped in rich cultural history, artistic heritage, and dynamic local traditions. From its famed porcelain industry to its awe-inspiring scenery and ancient sites, Jingdezhen offers travelers a unique blend of historical exploration, artistic appreciation, and natural beauty. As we reflect on the numerous dimensions of this intriguing city, it becomes evident that Jingdezhen is not simply a destination, but an experience, one that offers deeper insights into Chinese culture and an opportunity to connect with the heart of a centuries-old skill.

12.1 Final Thoughts on Jingdezhen as a Travel Destination

Jingdezhen is more than just a destination to visit; it's a place to experience and understand. The city's ancient origins in porcelain production have defined its identity, making it an important cultural and artistic hub in China. While many visitors come for its ceramic past, the city also provides lots of current attractions, including art galleries, picturesque places, and outdoor excursions. Whether you're admiring handcrafted pottery, hiking through verdant mountains, or eating local cuisines, Jingdezhen promises a varied and diverse vacation experience.

The warmth and hospitality of the inhabitants further enhance the experience, as they welcome guests into a world where tradition and innovation coexist. From the bustling workshops where artisans practice centuries-old traditions to the peaceful shrines and exuberant festivals, Jingdezhen captivates travelers with both its legacy and its present significance.

12.2 Reflections on the Blend of Tradition and Modernity

One of the most remarkable elements of Jingdezhen is how it merges traditional traditions with current innovations. The city's porcelain-making sector, stretching back over a thousand years, is a witness to the preservation of cultural customs. Yet, Jingdezhen is not locked in the past; it has adapted to the modern world in astonishing ways. Art museums and contemporary galleries present the works of both classic ceramicists and new artists who incorporate current techniques into their sculptures. The city has become a hub for foreign artists, students, and collectors who contribute to its ever-evolving ceramic culture.

This blend of old and contemporary may be evident in the architecture, where historic kiln sites coexist with sleek, modern buildings and international influences. The combination of old landmarks and contemporary architecture illustrates Jingdezhen's position as a city that honors its history while embracing the future. This dynamic blend makes it an appealing destination for people wishing to experience the best of both worlds.

12.3   Encouragement   to   Experience Jingdezhen for Yourself

Jingdezhen is a place that welcomes discovery. Whether you're a lover of history, art, nature, or culture, the city has plenty to offer. Travelers interested in the arts will find themselves fascinated by the myriad options to learn about porcelain production, take workshops, and purchase unique handmade ceramics. Natural lovers may explore the nearby mountains, rivers, and natural reserves, while those seeking cultural immersion can visit historic temples, and local markets, and participate in one of the many exciting festivals.

For first-time tourists, Jingdezhen allows stepping off the beaten road and exploring a side of China that is less commercialized but no less compelling. With its friendly population, rich past, and variety of things to see and do, it's easy to see why Jingdezhen is gaining popularity as a must-visit destination in China.

12.4 Closing Remarks and Travel Recommendations

In conclusion, Jingdezhen is a city that brilliantly integrates ancient traditions with modernity, delivering a travel experience that is both enriching and distinctive. Whether you're enthralled by the artistry of porcelain, intrigued by the city's historical significance, or simply searching for a calm vacation in nature, Jingdezhen has it all.

For those planning a trip, it is highly recommended to spend time seeing both the cultural landmarks and natural environs. Don't miss a visit to the famed porcelain workshops, historic kilns, and the many museums that chronicle the story of this magnificent city. Be sure to also explore the neighboring area, where gorgeous walks, picturesque villages, and outdoor activities await.

Jingdezhen is a place that will leave a lasting impact, allowing guests not just a glimpse into China's historic creative traditions but also the chance to experience the blooming inventiveness of a modern city. Whether you're a pottery aficionado, history buff, or adventure seeker, Jingdezhen guarantees an unforgettable experience that will stick with you long after your visit.